Olympic Spirit

Inspirational Stories from the Olympic Games

Scott Frothingham

Olympic Spirit

Other books by Scott Frothingham:

Olympic Gold
Olympic Gold #2
Mount Rushmore Motivation
6-Minute Success Training
Success-ercize

Published by
FastForwardPublishing.com

Photo Credits page 35

ISBN-10: 1494992604
ISBN-13: 978-1494992606

DEDICATION

This book is dedicated to sportscaster Jim McKay. For over 35 years, he was the voice of *ABC's Wide World of Sports* ("the thrill of victory and the agony of defeat") and he covered a dozen Olympics, including 16 straight hours when Palestinian terrorists kidnapped 11 Israeli Olympians during the 1972 Games that ended with his unforgettable words, "They're all gone". When I was growing up, he was the voice of the Olympics to me ... to this day, I can still hear his voice when I watch Olympic events. McKay died in 2008.

CONTENTS

INTRODUCTION — page 5

Story 1 - The Stubborn Champion — page 6

Story 2 - The Selfless Sailor — page 8

Story 3 - The Steadfast Skier — page 10

Story 4 - The Tenacious Diver — page 11

Story 5 - The Perceptive Runner — page 12

Story 6 - The Tough Teenager — page 14

Story 7 - The Persistent Swordsman — page 16

Story 8 - The Determined Ironman — page 18

Story 9 - The Unique Marksman — page 20

Story 10 - The Supportive Father — page 22

Celebrate Humanity — page 24

Olympic Gold — page 27

Olympic Gold #2 — page 28

BONUS Story - The Ultimate Fighter — page 29

About the Author — page 32

Request — page 33

Recommendation — page 34

Photo Credits — page 35

INTRODUCTION

What makes an inspiring Olympic moment? Is it the years of hard work and sacrifice that culminate in a gold medal? Is it suffering an injury but finishing the race? Is it overcoming a stereotype and proving something to the world? All these factors and more play a part in the great moments of Olympic history and give us stories that can motivate us in our business and personal lives. Here are 11 stories of Olympic Spirit.

Story 1 - The Stubborn Champion

Six days before competition was to begin in the 1964 Olympic games, USA discus thrower Al Oerter slipped on a wet concrete discus circle and tore rib cartilage on his right side – his throwing side – causing internal bleeding and severe pain.

Team doctors told him to forget the Games and not throw for at least 6-weeks. Oerter is quoted as responding, "This is the Olympics. You die before you quit."

A week later, Al Oerter broke the Olympic record and won the gold medal.

Oerter competed in 4 consecutive Olympic games, winning the gold medal each time – a sweep made all the more remarkable because in each case he broke the Olympic record AND in each case he had to overcome adversity and/or was not the favorite to win:

Melbourne 1956 - as an inexperienced 20-year-old, Oerter is considered a long shot for a medal and stuns the crowd by winning the gold medal with a record breaking 1st throw.

Rome 1960 - nearly killed in a 1957 automobile accident, Oerter is not expected to beat his teammate, friend, and world record holder, Rink Babka, who was leading the competition, but takes the gold with another Olympic record throw.

Tokyo 1964 - hampered by a rib injury (story above), on his 5th and final throw Oerter sets another Olympic record

Mexico City 1968 - not only do the majority of experts think he is too old, but the rest of the field is well ahead in distances ... and ... it starts to rain; Oerter wins and sets his final Olympic Discus Record.

Al Oerter was the first track and field athlete to win four successive Olympic titles, a feat since equaled only by Carl Lewis in the long jump and is still the only athlete to win the same Olympic event four times in a row setting Olympic records each time.

Story 2 - The Selfless Sailor

This is the story of Canadian sailor Larry Lemieux.

During the 1988 Olympics in Seoul, Lemieux was sailing alone near the halfway point in second place in the fifth of a seven-race event.

It suddenly became very windy, escalating from 15 to 35 knots. On a nearby course, 2 Singapore sailors in another race were thrown into the rough water. Injured, they were unable to right their damaged boat.

Upon seeing the capsized crew, Lemieux broke away from his race and sailed to rescue them. After rescuing and getting them to an official patrol boat, he rejoined his race and finished 22nd.

By going off course and saving the lives of those two men, Lemieux forfeited an almost certain medal.

But his selfless act did not go unrecognized: soon after the race, the jury of the International Yacht Racing Union unanimously decided that Lemieux should be awarded second place, the position he was in when he went to the aid of the Singapore crew. At the medal awards ceremony, Lemieux was awarded the Pierre de Coubertin Medal for Sportsmanship by International Olympic Committee president Juan Antonio Saramanch who said, "By your sportsmanship, self-sacrifice, and courage you embody all that is right with the Olympic ideal." At the time, Lemieux was only the fifth recipient of the de Coubertin Medal that was introduced in 1964.

Story 3 - The Steadfast Skier

The 2010 Olympics in Vancouver were underway and on February 17, during the warm-up for the 1.4K classic sprint, Slovenian cross country skier Petra Majdic skied off-course, down a bank, into a 10 ft deep gully where she crashed on rocks breaking both ski poles, a ski tip, and five ribs.

The start time for her qualifying round was pushed back, but she collapsed in pain after qualifying and was taken to hospital to be x-rayed. Since the x-rays failed to show the rib fractures, she returned to the course and, despite the agonizing pain, won her quarterfinal and got through the semifinal. During the semifinal, one of the broken ribs pierced her lung, collapsing it.

Despite this and the excruciating pain, she finished third to win the bronze medal in the final, the first individual Winter Olympic medal for Slovenia in 16 years.

Story 4 - The Tenacious Diver

It's the preliminary round for springboard in the 1988 Olympics in Seoul. Defending Olympic springboard champion Greg Louganis, arguably the best diver in the world, attempts a reverse two-and-a-half pike on his 9th dive.

Shockingly, his head hits the board and he falls into the water. Louganis is concussed and receives temporary sutures.

35 minutes later, Louganis is back to perform his last dive and registers the highest score awarded in the preliminaries.

Following the preliminary round, Louganis was taken to a hospital and where he got five stitches. The next day he won the gold medal and became the first diver in history to successfully defend his Olympic springboard title. Days later he won gold in the 10m event.

Story 5 - The Perceptive Runner

When Mongolian Pyambu Tuul started the marathon at the 1992 Barcelona Olympics, he was not expected to win a medal. And he performed as expected, falling back to the rear of the pack soon after the start of Games' most grueling event.

When Hwang Young-cho of Korea crossed after the line in 2 hours 13 minutes and 23 seconds to win the Gold medal, Tuul still was about two hours away from the stadium.

When he came in last, finishing the race a couple of minutes over four hours, a reporter asked him why he was so slow and he replied '"No, my time was not slow, after all you could call my run a Mongolian Olympic marathon record."

Then another reporter asked him whether it was the greatest day of his life and Tuul humbly offered this stunning response:

"And as for it being the greatest day of my life, no it isn't", he said,""Up till six months ago I had no sight at all. I was a totally blind person. When I trained it was only with the aid of friends who ran with me. But a group of doctors came to my country last year to do humanitarian medical work. One doctor took a look at my eyes and asked me questions. I told him I had been unable to see since childhood. He said 'But I can fix your sight with a simple operation'. So he did the operation on me and after 20 years I could see again. So today wasn't the greatest day of my life. The best day was when I got my sight back and I saw my wife and two daughters for the first time. And they are beautiful."

Story 6 - The Tough Teenager

The US women were on the verge of an historic win in the team competition in the 1996 Olympics in Atlanta. In the team competition, an event dominated by the Russians for decades and never won by the United States, the U.S. competed with the Russian, Romanian, and Ukrainian teams. The Russians came into the team competition with a very narrow lead. The event came down to the final rotation on the final day of the team competition, July 23, 1996.

Then the unthinkable happened: Dominique Moceanu, the youngest member of the team, fell on both of her vaults. With just a slim lead over the Russian team, it was essential that Kerri Strug, the final American gymnast to nail her vault. But Strug fell too, injuring her ankle in the process.

In the time interval between her two vaults, Strug asked, "Do we need this? Coach Béla Károlyi replied, "Kerri, we need you to go one more time. We need you one more time for the gold. You can do it..."

It was time for her next vault. Strug limped slightly to the end of the runway and, ignoring her injury, she ran down for another attempt. She landed the vault briefly on both feet, almost instantly hopping onto only her good foot, saluting the judges, assuring the Americans their first Olympic team gold. She then crumpled to her knees in pain, requiring assistance off the landing platform.

Later, coach Károlyi carried her onto the medals podium to join her team, after which she was treated at a hospital for a third-degree lateral sprain and tendon damage.

NOTE: Due to her injury, Strug was unable to compete in the individual all-around competition and event finals, despite having qualified for both

Story 7 - The Persistent Swordsman

He had won a bronze medal in the 1988 Summer Olympics and was the top ranked fencer in the world; At 27 years old, Pal Szekeres was living his dream. Then his world came tumbling down in a bus accident that left him with a serious spinal injury and confined to a wheelchair.

An early end to a successful, albeit brief athletic career. No. Maybe the end of one part of an athletic career, but the beginning of a new one. Because Szekeres still wanted to compete. And compete, he did, going on to win 3 gold and 3 bronze medals in the Paralympic Games.

"It is still fencing, whether you are standing or sitting," he said.

Pal Szekeres is the only athlete to have won medals at both the Olympic and Paralympic Games.

"For me, it's the same success either as an Olympian or a Paralympian. I'm a fencer and I'm proud of my Olympic bronze and my Paralympic medals."

NOTE: Before the Paralympics, American gymnast George Eyser, who had a wooden leg, competed at the 1904 Summer Olympics, and won three gold medals, two silver and a bronze, including a gold in the vault, an event which then included a jump over a long horse without aid of a springboard. Other amputee medalists at the Olympic Games prior to the creation of the Paralympics include Oliver Halassy of Hungary, whose left leg was amputated below the knee, won three medals (two gold and a silver) in water polo, in 1928, 1932 and 1936 and Karoly Takacs, also of Hungary, won gold in shooting at the 1948 Summer Olympics (his right hand had been "shattered by a grenade" ten years earlier, and he had taught himself to shoot with his left). Also, deaf Hungarian fencer Ildikó Újlaky-Rejtő won two individual medals (a gold and a bronze) and five team medals at the Olympics between 1960 and 1976. Although her Olympic career coincided with the beginning of the Paralympics, she never competed in it.

Story 8 - The Determined Iron Man

In the 1960s and 70s, the Japanese built a dynasty in men's gymnastics; by the 1976 Olympics in Montreal, Japan had won the team gold in the last four Olympics.

In the team finals in Montreal, however, on the final tumble of his floor routine, Japanese team member Shun Fujimoto broke his kneecap. Fearing that the team would not win if he withdrew from the meet, Fujimoto hid the extent of his injury and competed in his final two events of the day: pommel horse and rings.

He scored 9.5 on the pommel horse and then, still hiding the pain from the broken knee, moved on to the rings. "I knew that if my posture was not good on landing, I would not receive a good score. I knew I must try to forget the pain". In his dismount, he pulled a twisting triple somersault, later admitting "the pain went through me like a knife". He landed with a perfect finish, grimacing as his knee buckled slightly, and, with tears in eyes, raising his arms high before collapsing in agony. He scored 9.7, his best ever result.

The dismount worsened his injury, dislocating his broken kneecap and tearing ligaments in his right leg. Doctors ordered him to withdraw from further competition or risk permanent disability. One doctor stated: "How he managed to do somersaults and twists and land without collapsing in screams is beyond my comprehension."

Now a man short, the Japanese team were inspired to gold by his sacrifice.

Story 9 - The Unique Marksman

By the time Korean archer Im Dong Hyun had reached his mid-twenties, he was considered to be one of the finest archers in the world. Although he has not won an individual Olympic medal, he had helped his team win gold medals in 2004 in Athens and 2008 in Beijing and the bronze medal in 2012 in London. At the 2012 Summer Olympics he set a new world record score of 699 for the 72-arrow event. He had also won team and individual gold medals in the World Championships, the World Cup and the Asian Games. And in May 2012, he broke his own world record at the World Cup with a score of 696.

Impressive accomplishments, especially when it is revealed that Im Dong Hyun is LEGALLY BLIND.

Hyun suffers from myopia, which has left him with 20/100 vision in his right eye and 20/200 vision in his left eye, that designates him as legally blind.

Think about it, a blind man who successfully shoots arrows across great distances into incredibly small targets without being able to see those targets.

"With my vision, when I look at the target, it looks as if different color paints have been dropped in water," IM says. "When I look down the range at the target all I can do is try to distinguish between the different colors. If I couldn't see the colors, now that would be a problem."

This remarkable competitor apparently does not like the attention that is blurry vision receives. I don't have a stick, I don't have a blind dog," he said. "It's unpleasant when people say I'm disabled."

Story 10 - The Supportive Father

Even though his track and field career had been plagued by injuries, Britain's Derek Redmond was expected to compete for a medal in the 400-meter race in the 1992 Olympics in Barcelona.

The stadium is packed with 65,000 fans to watch the semifinal 400 heat. The race begins and Redmond breaks from the pack and takes the lead.

But with 175 meters to go, Redmond pulls a hamstring and hobbles a few steps and falls to his knees in tears ... his dream of an Olympic medal ended.

But that's just the beginning of this story; what happened next is still, for millions of sports fans, a moment that it etched in their minds and hearts as one of the most emotional moments in the history of athletics.

Crying, Redmond gets himself upright to try to finish the race on one leg. The race is over and the crowd realizes that Redmond is going to attempt to finish the race. Recognizing the athlete's pride and heart, the crowd rises and beings to cheer.

As Redmond painfully limps onward, the roar of the crowd grows louder. About 120 meters from the finish line, an unidentified man, undeterred by race officials trying to stop him, makes his way to the track to help support the athlete. It's Redmond's father.

Supported by his father, Jim, who waves off help, Redmond makes it to a few feet from the finish line where his father releases his grip so Redmond could cross the finish line by himself. Then Jim throws his arms back around Derek crying (as is the crowd in the stadium and those watching on TV).

What Derek Redmond said:

> "I wasn't doing it for the crowd, I was doing it for me. Whether people thought I was an idiot or a hero, I wanted to finish the race. I'm the one who has to live with it."

and

> "Everything I had worked for was finished. I hated everybody. I hated the world. I hated hamstrings. I hated it all. I felt so bitter that I was injured again. I told myself I had to finish. I kept hopping round. Then, with 100 metres to go, I felt a hand on my shoulder. It was my old man."

What Jim Redmond said:

> "I'm the proudest father alive, I'm prouder of him than I would have been if he had won the gold medal. It took a lot of guts for him to do what he did."

Celebrate Humanity

Before and during the 2000 Olympic Games in Sydney, Australia, the International Olympic Committee ran a promotional program designed to communicate the core values of the Olympic Games: "Celebrate Humanity". Translated into 18 languages, the campaign ran on media around the world.

Academy Award winning actor and comedian Robin Williams who narrated the English version of the campaign said, "Many of my favorite Olympic memories were not gold medal situations. They were inspiring moments of humanity that transcended borders, obstacles and languages--and unified people around the world. I feel this campaign conveys that, and I am proud to be a part of it."

Here are transcripts of the narration of 6 of the promotional announcement that were part of the IOC's "Celebrate Humanity":

Courage

Strength is measured in pounds.
Speed is measured in seconds.
Courage...
You can't measure courage.

Bronze

Just a reminder:
At the Olympic Games
You don't have to come in first
To win.

Giant

To be a giant.
This has forever been our passion,
this desire to be a giant.
Not to stand on one's shoulders or have one for a friend,
Though these may be fortunate things,
But to be one.
Giants step over barriers that seem never-ending.
They conquer mountains that appear insurmountable,
Giants rise above fear,
Triumph over pain,
Push themselves and inspire others
To be a Giant,
To do Giant things,
To take Giant steps,
To move the world forward.

Silver

Someone once said,
"You don't win the silver,
You lose the gold."
Obviously...
They never won the silver.

Rhymes

They gather together, thousands and thousands and thousands
still more
For sixteen straight days the stadiums roar
They line all the fields, they polish the courts
A rainbow of colors together for sport
They sprint, they jostle, they jump, they shout
They sometimes get hostile but they work it all out
They smile, they laugh, they learn life's lessons
They respect one another regardless of weapons
The big and the small together seem awkward
but amazingly enough they push the world forward
And when it's all over it's as good as it gets
A lifetime of memories with zero regrets
Then they pack up the balls and roll up the mats
Put on their best suits and the finest of hats
They all wave goodbye, they hug and they kiss
And you think, that maybe, just maybe, it could all be like
this

Adversary

You are my adversary, but you are not my enemy.
For your resistance gives me strength,
Your will gives me courage,
Your spirit ennobles me.
And though I aim to defeat you, should I succeed, I will not
humiliate you.
Instead, I will honor you.
For without you, I am a lesser man.

Olympic Gold

Here are 5 quotes from Olympic Medal winners on the Olympic Spirit (selected from the 140+ quotes in the book "*Olympic Gold*")

"The greatest memory for me of the 1984 Olympics was not the individual honors, but standing on the podium with my teammates to receive our team gold medal." -Mitch Gaylord, 4 time Olympic medalist - gymnastics

"I didn't set out to beat the world; I just set out to do my absolute best." -Al Oerter, 4 time Olympic medalist - track and field

"It is the inspiration of the Olympic Games that drives people not only to compete but to improve, and to bring lasting spiritual and moral benefits to the athlete and inspiration to those lucky enough to witness the athletic dedication." - Herb Elliott, 1 time Olympic medalist - track and field

"We all have dreams. But in order to make dreams come into reality, it takes an awful lot of determination, dedication, self-discipline, and effort." -Jesse Owens, 4 time Olympic medalist - track and field

"At the two-thirds mark, I think of those who are still with me. Who might a break? Should I? Then I give it all I've got." -Ibrahim Hussein, 2 Olympic Games- track and field

Olympic Gold #2

Here are 5 quotes from Olympic Medal winners on the Olympic Spirit (selected from the 140+ quotes in the book *"Olympic Gold #2"*)

"My dad would tell me to, 'Play for those who couldn't play.' So my motivation is for people who struggle in life daily." -Misty May-Treanor, 3 time Olympic medalist - beach volleyball

"When I go out on the ice, I just think about my skating. I forget it is a competition." -Katarina Witt, figure skater, 2 time Olympic medalist

"When I go out and race, I'm not trying to beat opponents, I'm trying to beat what I have done ... to beat myself, basically. People find that hard to believe because we've had such a bias to always strive to win things. If you win something and you haven't put everything into it, you haven't actually achieved anything at all. When you've had to work hard for something and you've got the best you can out of yourself on that given day, that's where you get satisfaction from." - Ian Thorpe, 9 time Olympic medalist - swimming

"Gold medals are made out of your sweat, blood, and tears." - Gabby Douglas, 2 time Olympic medalist - gymnastics

"Failure I can live with. Not trying is what I can't handle!" -Sanya Richards-Ross, 5 time Olympic medalist - track and field

BONUS STORY: The Ultimate Fighter

Perhaps the most dramatic, and anticipated moment of the Olympic Opening Ceremony is the arrival of the Olympic flame and the lighting of the Olympic flame. And perhaps the most emotional and inspiring arrival/lighting occurred in 1996 in Atlanta.

For the Atlanta Olympics, the torch arrived in the United States 84 days before the start of the games (together with the 16 days of competition it will add up to a symbolic 100 days) and traveled more than 16,000 miles. An estimated 3.5 billion people around the world, along with the assembled athletes watched the arrival of the flame, curious who the final torch bearer would be.

The final runner, four-time discus gold-medal winner Al Oerter, arrives at the stadium and ignites the torch held by three-time heavyweight world champion boxer Evander Holyfield who enters the stadium and is joined by Greek runner Voula Patoulidou and the two of them carry the torch around the stadium track and pass the torch to US swimmer Janet Evans.

As Beethoven's "Ode to Joy" is played Evans takes her lap around the track towards the long ramp leading up to the top of the stadium. The cheers from the capacity crowd crescendo.

All eyes are on Evans as she climbs the ramp. Then, at the top of the stadium they are treated to a surprise. At the top of the ramp is "The Greatest", the incomparable Muhammad Ali.

The crowd gasps and then joins together in a tumultuous roar The heavyweight boxing gold medalist at the 1960 Olympics in Rome and regarded by many to be the greatest professional heavyweight boxing champion of all time, Ali is one of the most recognizable sports figures worldwide.

Evans touches her torch to Ali's, igniting it. Ali holds the Olympic torch unsteadily in his right hand while his left shakes uncontrollably with the symptoms of Parkinson's disease. He raises the flame and is met with supportive cheers from the elated audience.

Watching Muhammad Ali proudly hold the Olympic torch, despite his crippling ailment, stands as a great moment in sport, Olympics and beyond. The world was inspired by a man recognized as a great fighter during his boxing days as he continued to fight, this time his crippling ailment.

A Sports Illustrated picture of the scene was entitled: "The greatest start to an Olympics."

US President Bill Clinton, who was there to open the Olympic Games said, "That took a sackful of guts...and it's taken a lot of courage to continue to go out, to be seen...he wasn't self-conscious. He's something special."

The emotional and inspirational moment of Muhammad Ali lighting the stadium cauldron to open the 1996 Atlanta Olympic Games has become an iconic image in Olympic history.

For the dignity of the man was consummate – never relinquishing ideals for money or fame, Ali was the people's champion – the underdog in sport and life. "They didn't tell me who would light the flame, but when I saw it was you, I cried" said Bill Clinton. He wasn't the only one.

ABOUT THE AUTHOR

Scott Frothingham is an entrepreneur, consultant, speaker, business coach and author best known for his FastForward Income™ products including *The 15-minute Sales Workout™*. He helps entrepreneurs, managers and sales/marketing executives position themselves for success through skills training and personal development -- along with providing tools for effectively and efficiently training and motivating their teams.

 Some of Scott's other books authored by include "Olympic Gold", "Olympic Gold #2", "Success-ercize" and the 6 book "Words and Wisdom" series featuring great Americans such as Abraham Lincoln, Ben Franklin, Teddy Roosevelt and Mark Twain.

www.ScottFrothingham.com
Facebook: www.Facebook.com/FastForwardIncome
Twitter: **@ScottFroth**

A Request

Can I Ask a Favor?

Thank you so much for reading my book. I hope you really liked it.

As you probably know, many people look at the reviews on Amazon before they decide to purchase a book.

If you liked the book, **could you please take a minute** to leave a review with your feedback?

Just go to Amazon.com, look up *Olympic Spirit - Frothingham* go to the book's page and scroll down until you see the orange "Write a customer review button", click it and write a few words about why you like the book.

 A couple of minutes is all I'm asking for, and it would mean the world to me.

Thank you so much,
Scott

Recommendation

For your business or personal success library

Available on Amazon.com and from other retailers

Photo Credits

Cover: Tring - Beacon to welcome the Paralympics Torch ©
Copyright Rob Farrow Licensed under the Creative Commons
Attribution-Share Alike 2.0 Generic license

Olympic Sports Pictograms : Parutakupiu 19 November; derivatives:
Tomtheman5 2006 Public domain

www.FastForwardPublishing.com

26612764R00022

Made in the USA
Middletown, DE
03 December 2015